Work from Home Amazon Book 1

$10,000 per Month from Amazon - 5 Ways: Amazon FBA, etc.

book has been derived from various sources. Please consult a licensed professional before attempting any techniques outlined in this book.

By reading this document, the reader agrees that under no circumstances is the author responsible for any losses, direct or indirect, which are incurred as a result of the use of information contained within this document, including, but not limited to, —errors, omissions, or inaccuracies.

Table of Contents

My other book on how to work from home:

«Work from home: $10,000 per Month. Proven Case Studies»: https://www.amazon.com/dp/B07FQCF449

Introduction

I want to thank you for choosing this book, '*Work from home Amazon Book 1 - $10,000 per month from Amazon - 5 ways: Amazon FBA, etc.*'

We live in a world where there are numerous unique business opportunities. Gone are the days of earning a living from traditional business ventures. The e-commerce industry has revolutionized the concept of finance and commerce altogether, and Amazon is one such venture. This multinational tech-based company focuses on e-commerce, cloud computing, artificial intelligence and digital streaming. It is considered to be among the Big Four technology companies in league with Facebook, Google, and Apple.

In this book, you will learn about five ways in which you can use Amazon to generate $10,000 per month. The five different options discussed include selling a product using Amazon's FBA, private labeling a product, retail arbitrage, working as a delivery fulfillment warehouse associate, and joining Amazon Flex.

So, let us get started without further ado!

Chapter One: Sell a Product Using Amazon's FBA

Amazon offers a 2-day free shipping policy through Amazon Price. This has become one of the main reasons why a lot of online shoppers are attracted to Amazon. If you want to become a seller, then leveraging this 2-day free shipping on items you wish to sell is a great resource to have in your arsenal.

By using Amazon FBA (Fulfillment by Amazon), you will need to ship your products listed on Amazon to their warehouses, and they will do the rest of the work for you. For instance, if you ship a box of 25 items you wish to sell to the Amazon warehouse, the Amazon logistics team will pick it up, pack and then ship those items to the final consumers as and when you sell them on Amazon. It is a cost-effective means of shipping your items, and by paying a fee for this service, you will provide your customers with effective industry-leading logistics for making sure their packages are delivered on time. The main benefits of using FBA are that the Amazon team will pick and pack your products, store and ship them and also provide the necessary customer support.

In 2008, two college students started Etailz as part of a project for their college curriculum regarding how to sell on Amazon. They managed to generate a revenue of over $90 million by 2015. This multimillion-dollar empire started with college students who wanted to sell their products on Amazon! Also, Etailz was invited by Amazon Canada to be their first FBA seller in 2013.

Different Stages of the FBA Program

The first stage is to find the product you wish to sell. You can start by a simple Amazon search for the Amazon Best Sellers list to get an idea of all the best-selling products. The product you want to sell must be light and relatively small. Ideally, you must be able to sell it for over $10, it must not be easily breakable, and you must be interested in selling it too. You can also use an online platform like AMZScout to find the best products on Amazon.

The next step is to source the product you want to sell. You can source it using a website like Alibaba, by visiting local exhibitions or even Google to find suppliers of the products you wish to sell.

Then you need to create your account and product listing. You will learn more about this in the subsequent section.

Once you have the product ready, you need to ship it to the Amazon warehouse near you. This is an option available exclusively to FBA sellers. After this, it is time to start selling.

Steps to Start Selling using FBA

Step one: Creating a seller account

To create an Amazon Seller account, simply click on this **link: https://services.amazon.com/content/sell-on-amazon.html** Click on the "Start Selling" option to create your seller profile on Amazon. Please go through. Click on the "Start Selling" option to create your seller profile on Amazon. Please go through the "Before you register" portion of the website before you decide to start selling. There are two kinds of Seller accounts to choose from, and they are Professional and Individual. If you are planning to sell over 40 items per month, then opt for the Professional account or else opt for the Individual account. Amazon charges you $0.99 per item when you use an Individual account, and it costs $39.99 to opt for the Professional plan. If you opt for the Professional plan, you can sell unlimited products by paying the required fee.

You must include information regarding your business name, address, your contact number, the method of billing, and tax information (if you opt for the Professional account).

Before you go further, print this agreement by clicking on the link given in the window. This will help you in future reference. Then agree to the terms and conditions of the agreement and proceed further. First off, you will need to provide your credit card details and billing address, followed by your seller name and business address.

Step two: Amazon Seller Central

You need to create a product listing. To do this, you must take high-quality images of the items you want to list on Amazon, write their product descriptions, include the keywords related to those items, and create your listing.

For adding products, open your Seller Account, go to "Inventory" and click on the "Add a Product" option. Include information like the selling price of the item, the item's condition, and whether you want Amazon to ship the item or not. After you do this, you need to convert the items to FBA items. To do this, follow these steps: Inventory ☐ Manage Inventory ☐ Actions ☐ Click on the Fulfilled by Amazon option. If you wish to sell new items, then you can opt for the "Stickerless and Commingled Inventory" option. The FBA Label Service allows Amazon to place their label on your items, and you don't have to do this.

Step three: Shipment plan

You need to create a shipping plan. Once you add the second item to your list, you must create a shipping plan. To do this, select the address you want to ship the product from and the type of packing. The two packing options are "Case-packed products" and "Individual products." If you wish to send a box containing the same type of item in it, then opt for the former like when you wish to sell 30 Anchorman DVDs. After shipping plan is ready, you must add the products from your inventory to the same.

Now that your shipping plan is ready, you must ship the items by following this sequence: Inventory ☐ Manage FBA Shipments ☐ Continue with the Shipping Plan.

Please enter the number of units you wish to send and if any prep is required (either you can do this yourself or opt for Amazon to do the same). Once your shipment is ready, you must weigh the package and send it to the Amazon Fulfillment Center.

Step four: Start selling

Once you ship the products to Amazon and they have received it, your products will now be available for sale on Amazon. You merely need to wait for the customers to start buying your products now. As soon as someone wants to buy a product you listed, the same will be shipped out from the fulfillment warehouse to the customer.

Apart from this, if you want to sell on Amazon and want to be successful while doing so, read Amazon's rules and regulations thoroughly. If you don't follow the rules, you could ruin the opportunity of a lifetime and also risk losing your seller license. Pick a strategy and stick to it. But with certain conditions, a seller must adapt and act accordingly. If you are down on sales count, you can place an item for sale under a discount. Similarly, if you want to earn profits, look toward raising your prices on certain products that are in demand. The increment or decrement can be of the slightest value, but even it could have a more substantial influence on your income.

By following these simple steps, you can start earning over $10,000 per month. However, to get there, you need some time, patience, and work consistently toward your goal.

Chapter Two: Private Label your Product

When a company creates certain goods and services, but then the same is branded and sold by another company, it is referred to as private labeling. Amazon's Amazon Essentials, Walmart's Great Value, and Target's Mainstays are examples of private label products.

Step one: Find Products

The first step to private labeling products is to find products the same. If you want to start your own online business, then selling private label products through Amazon's FBA is a brilliant option. It is quite easy, and there are multiple tools you can use. So, start by brainstorming product ideas. Whenever you go to the store and are scanning through products, look for interesting products you can sell. Another place to look for ideas is Amazon. Go through different departments and subcategories while looking for new products and go through the "Hot New Releases" section in each department. You can also go through the bestselling products and make up your mind. Kickstarter and IndieGoGo are two sites worth checking out while scouting for product ideas. By selecting the right idea and pricing it well, you can easily start earning over $10,000.

Step two: Product attributes

Here are some qualities you must keep in mind while selecting products for private labeling.

The product must be small (around 8 11/16" X 5 7/16" X 1 3/4") and must not weigh more than a pound or two. Try to pick non-seasonal products since your earnings depend on the products you choose. Select products that are unregulated and are uncomplicated to use.

Step three: Necessary market research

Once you like the products you think you can sell as a private label, it is time to conduct a little market research to determine whether it is good enough to sell or not. You can use an app like the Jungle Scout's Chrome Extension to help with the market research. Open Amazon and search for your desired product, click on the "JS" button on your browser. You can go through the product's data like the average monthly sales and product reviews to understand whether the product is an effective option or not. While searching for products, select something where you can sell at least 100 units per month. Also, the product you opt for must not have too much competition, so look for good products with less than 100 reviews.

Step four: Suppliers and manufacturers

Now that you have a viable product idea, you need to start looking for suppliers or manufacturers. One of the best websites to use while scouting for potential suppliers and manufacturers is Alibaba. To find prospective suppliers on Alibaba, you must first create a buyer's profile, search for the product you want, find the product listings similar to the one you want to create and contact the supplier or manufacturer for more information. Different things you can inquire about are the terms of payment if the product can be customized, the price per unit for bulk orders, and if a sample can be shipped to your address.

Step five: Logo, design, and packing

You can put your logo on the product as well as the product's packing. You can design the logo yourself or hire someone for the same. Try to make your products look different from those of your competitors. Customization can be as simple as varying the color or a specific feature or design of the product. Good packing can help improve the customer experience. If you have an official website or a social networking page, you can include these details on the packing to create brand awareness.

Step six: Fulfillment strategy

You can rely on a fulfillment service like Amazon FBA for logistics and shipment support you need. You merely need to ship the inventory to Amazon, and they will take care of the items getting delivered to your customers.

Step seven: Listing

Once you have the inventory you need on hand; the next step is to ship it to the nearest Amazon fulfillment center. It might take anywhere between 4 to six weeks to do all this. In the meanwhile, you can use this time to create your product listings. While creating a listing on Amazon, you must ensure that everything you need is ready, including the stock of items you want to list on Amazon. The next thing to include is good-quality photographs of the items you wish to sell along with catchy and interesting product descriptions of each item. Use certain keywords while describing the product and in its title.

Once you do all this, you merely need to wait for the buyers to start purchasing.

One of the most successful private label products on Amazon is Card Against Humanity. This card game is amongst the funniest and popular toy sold on Amazon with over $1.5 million as sales. The essential takeaway from this success story is a product doesn't have to be backed by a strong brand to become successful. As long as the idea is engaging and the product is of good quality, you can become successful. The second one is that pre-marketing and marketing are essential to increase the buzz about a product and giving out samples and advertising to an email list are good ideas.

The owner of Feedbackz became a millionaire using private labeling on Amazon FBA. He suggests that to become a successful seller, you must introduce your product to the market as quickly as you can and start selling it quickly to show its viability. The three areas he concentrated on are obtaining more reviews, optimizing the listings, and legitimating his packaging and listings.

Angie Chacon, like a lot of other private-label sellers on Amazon, was looking for a means to escape from an extremely demanding and hectic full-time corporate job. She sought online selling as her way out of the clutches of her demanding job. She worked diligently and created Momma Moon Boutique, an online brand. She created her line of products for babies and kids based on the products she used for her children. She was selling only five products but managed to earn over $50,000 per month within six months and achieved the financial freedom to quit her 9-5 job.

A single product can help turn things around, and this stands true for Paul Reavey or Mr. Paul. The product he decided to sell was a hairbrush. He sourced over 200 hairbrushes from an AliExpress supplier for $370 including the shipping costs. He used this product to start his private-selling label and managed to earn over $2000 as sales. You can always use this as inspiration while getting started with private labeling on Amazon.

Chapter Three: Retail Arbitrage

Did you know that you could make millions by raiding the clearance racks on Walmart or Target and then reselling the same on Amazon? Well, Ryan Grant did this and started raking in six-figure profits within no time. He is a 28-year old who quit his accounting job and decided to opt for making money through retail arbitrage.

Retail arbitrage is a straightforward concept- you purchase products (like the ones from the clearance or sales aisles) for a specific price and then resell them online at a higher price. To get started with retail arbitrage, the first thing you must do is set up a seller account on Amazon. You need this account to access the app to start searching for items you can sell on Amazon. Start with an Individual seller account since it doesn't have any payable fees. Once you think you can sell more than 40 items per month, you can switch to the Professional account.

Once you have created your seller account, please download the Amazon Seller App. This app is free and is available on Amazon. You can obtain details like the selling price, fees and shipment time, among other details of a specific product listed on Amazon. You can use this app to scan the barcode of a product, and it will show you details about the same. You can use the Fulfillment by Amazon's Revenue Calculator to get the fee details for specific items. You need to enter the price, the cost of shipping it to Amazon, and the cost of the product. Once you enter these details, the tool will display the fees payable per product and the reasonable profit you can make from the product.

Now, you must make a list of stores you can use to gather the products for your retail arbitrage venture on Amazon. A couple of different stores you can visit are Staples, TJ Maxx, Walmart, Home Depot, Models' Sporting Goods, Target, and any other retail outlet stores of your choice. After you do all this, you need to look for products to sell. Make a list of items you think you can sell, visit the local retail store, open the Amazon Seller App, and start using it to scan the barcodes of products you wish to sell. Once you scan the product, the app will show you the information about the same. There are two things you must check for, and they are:

Whether the product can be sold on Amazon or not?

If yes, then what is the sales rank of the product? The sales rank provided by Amazon informs you about how quickly a specific item is selling on Amazon. As a rule of thumb, the lower the number, the better it is. Look for products whose sales ranks are lower than 250,000 at least for your first couple of products. Once you gain experience and become a confident seller, then you can tweak this number. If the app displays you are eligible for selling an item and the rank is within the limit you are looking at; then you must check if the product gives a favorable return on investment (ROI) or not. Click on the "Gross Proceeds" section of the app to check this value, input the selling price, the shipment cost (cost per pound) and the purchase cost.

If the numbers displayed seem favorable, then you have got yourself a clear winner. There are two things you must check now, and they are:

- Whether the net profit is higher than the average profit threshold or not.

- If yes, then calculate the ROI.

While getting started with retail arbitrage, you must ensure that you can earn at $3 as profit per item you sell. If the profit margin is lower than $3, then even the slightest drop in the selling price can eat into your profits. If the product helps you earn over $3, then you need to calculate the ROI percentage. To do this, you must divide the net profit by the cost of acquiring the item. For instance, the cost price is $7, and you are earning a profit of $3, then the ROI percentage is 70%. The ROI percentage you must look for must be at least 50% or higher if you want to stay profitable.

If an item meets all these requirements, then the next step is to purchase at least six units of that item. If you notice there are only six units available, then buy them all.

You must repeat all these steps for every product you might wish to sell. You must not skip any steps and go through them carefully. If a product doesn't meet any of the criteria, then move ahead. It must fit all the criteria, and there are no exceptions. So, it is wonderful that you are aware of the products you want to sell. Now, you must start pricing them. While selling on Amazon using FBA, you can look at the current pricing of similar items by other sellers to determine an ideal price. Try to set the price such that it matches the lowest price of the concerned product on Amazon. You can price the product anywhere up to 1% higher than the least price it is listed at on Amazon. For instance, if the lowest price for a product on Amazon is $45, then you can sell it for any price up to $49.50.

Once you have decided on the selling price of the item, the next step is to start shipping them to the nearest Amazon warehouse. Once you do this, the FBA service will take care of the rest for you. The steps to follow while shipping the products to the Amazon warehouse are the same as the previous sections.

Will Tirenlund decided to leverage a common experience and turned it into a profitable venture. A lot of college students are well versed with spending exorbitant prices to purchase the necessary textbooks. Well, Will realized the expenses involved and decided to turn this into a profitable business venture. He used to buy books and started to sell them at a price lower than the ones at a regular university bookstore.

This gave him the necessary experience to gather an inventory. He soon started to order the necessary inventory at lower costs from China and started to sell this under their brand name.

Larry Lubarsky was once in significant debt and was unemployed too. However, today, he is a successful owner of a small business earning millions of dollars by selling on Amazon. Lubrasky sources items in bulk from different sellers belonging to different departments ranging from electronics to health supplies and then resells the same on Amazon. For instance, if he sources a nerf gun for $10 from a wholesaler and resells it $20, he ends up with a net profit of $5. It is a very simple strategy that anyone can use to become a successful seller on Amazon.

Chapter Four: Work as a Delivery Fulfillment Warehouse Associate

Working as a delivery fulfillment warehouse associate at Amazon can be quite rewarding. Also, this is a great way to earn a part-time income. You can work anywhere between 15 to 24-hours per week at a minimum pay of $15 per hour.

Regardless of whether you want a part-time, full-time, flex, or seasonal employment, Amazon can help earn money. Every member of the Amazon team helps fulfill the orders and make global customers as well as sellers happy. There are different jobs available, and you can become a part of the Amazon Fulfillment team by opting for any of the following.

By opting to work in the Fulfillment Centers, you will essentially be working inside an Amazon warehouse. You will be a part of the team that's responsible for selecting, packing, and shipping the orders you receive. If a fast-paced job with physical job profile that gets you up and about, then this might work well for you. You will be given a preset full-time work schedule.

Amazon's Delivery Station is the final pit stop before a specific order is shipped out for delivery to the customer's address. This is an active job wherein you will need to sort packages according to delivery routes to ensure Amazon can fulfill its delivery guarantee.

You can work part-time and opt for early morning or late-night shifts where each shift lasts for anywhere between 4 to 6 hours.

The Amazon's Sort Center is the first pit stop an item makes on its journey from the warehouse. This is not a small job and is an essential part of the journey a product makes from the time an order is placed until its delivery. If you wish to apply to this job, then ensure that you don't mind being up and about sorting packages between delivery trucks.

Amazon's Prime Now is a service which offers quick delivery within two or less than two-hours for certain products. By opting to work in the Prime Now Warehouse, you will be working closely with a small team and will be responsible for packing and getting the products ready for delivery within an hour.

The Amazon Fresh Warehouse is Amazon's grocery delivery service. It offers fresh, packaged, and frozen groceries that you need to gather, pack and organize for the perfect delivery and order fulfillment.

To apply, please go to Amazon Jobs or click on this **link: https://www.amazon.jobs/en-gb** Once you do this, you can either select the option "Job Application" present on the top right corner of the screen or click on the "Fulfillment Center Hiring" option on the screen. After you do this, you merely need to check for jobs in your chosen area, ensure you have the necessary qualifications and apply. You don't need a resume or even attend an interview to join Amazon's team of warehouse fulfillment associates. You merely need to complete the application process by following the above-mentioned steps. Once you do this, you must select a date and get ready to work.

The only two requirements are that you must be at least 18 years or older and need a high-school diploma or any other equivalent qualification. As long as you fulfill these two requirements, you can work for Amazon.

Chapter Five: Amazon Flex

Amazon spent over $21 billion on shipping costs in the year 2017. The good news is you can get a slice of this action by joining Amazon Flex. Amazon Flex is Amazon's in-house courier service and helps outsource services of delivery to all those customers who are subscribers of Amazon.com, AmazonFresh, Prime Now, and Amazon Restaurants.

Amazon is primarily hiring drivers for delivering packages as part of the Amazon Flex program that allows customers to receive their orders within an hour or two. As long as you manage to complete the delivery within the given time, have a vehicle you can use and a smartphone, you can start earning anywhere between $15 and $25 per hour.

Join Amazon Flex

The jobs available depend on your location along with the need for delivery services in that area. The first step is to open the **Amazon Flex: https://flex.amazon.com/get-s?tag=aboutcom02thebalance-20website** and go through the available job openings. If there is nothing available at the moment, then you can sign-up and place yourself on Amazon's waitlist.

There are specific qualifications you need to join Amazon Flex, and they are as follows:

You must be at least 21 years or older and must be a holder of a valid US driver's license. The Amazon Flex app asks different questions before you can become a part of the Flex team like the details of your driving record, whether you have any criminal record or not along with basic questions for your background check. It can take up to 5 days to receive the approval if you qualify. To be a part of Amazon Flex, you need to be willing to use your own vehicle (Amazon even allows the use of bicycles in some regions). According to different locations, you might require a car for the necessary cargo space. You must ensure the vehicle's registration and insurance documents are in order. The final requirement is a smartphone for downloading the Amazon Flex app for schedule and delivering the orders.

Get Started

Download the app and complete the necessary paperwork to get started. Only after you fulfill all the requirements set by Amazon Flex will you be able to start making deliveries. The first step is to download the Amazon Flex app, fill the questionnaire the app provides along with information about your banking details to get paid. Once you do this, and your paperwork is complete, you must establish your schedule.

The app will give you the list of different slots according to the orders available in the form of 3-6 hour shifts. The app will provide shifts according to the hours you want to work. Also, if you don't grab an available slot offer on the app, some other driver can accept it. Check the "Available Blocks" section in the app for any same-day delivery opportunities.

After you book your slot, it is time to start driving. An hour before your shift starts, you will get a notification on the app reminding you about the upcoming shift and the pickup locations for all the deliveries. Once you get to the location, it is time to check-in and start your shift. Use your smartphone's camera to scan the barcode on the items to be included in the delivery route as you are loading them into your vehicle. According to the cargo space available in the vehicle, you can carry the packages. Once you do all this and are ready to start driving, you can use the app to navigate yourself to the delivery locations. After arriving at the location, check whether the customer has listed any delivery instructions like leaving the item on the doorstep, not ringing the doorbell or using a specific gate code. Before you hand over the package, you must rescan the barcode to mark the completion of the delivery. Time management is quintessential while you are trying to complete the deliveries within your scheduled block. Amazon Flex might not pay you if you are delayed because of some reason or the other if the packages you were supposed to deliver within your scheduled block are undelivered.

The risk of running out of time is a part of joining Amazon Flex. However, you do have the chance to earn as much as $150 per day, excluding any tips you receive from the customers. You are eligible for receiving payments twice per week according to the days you work.

Conclusion

I want to thank you for purchasing this book.

Now that you are aware of different ways you can earn money by using Amazon, it is time to select an option and get started. Pick an option according to your preferences, convenience, and goals. Once you do this, you need to create your account with the platform and start making the most of the services offered by Amazon. By using Amazon's services, you can start earning over $10,000. All that you must do is carefully consider your options, work diligently, and be patient.

Thank you and all the best!

Resources

https://www.nchannel.com/blog/how-to-sell-on-amazon-for-beginners-using-fba/

https://www.bigcommerce.com/blog/amazon-private-label-products/#how-to-find-and-sell-private-label-products

https://startupbros.com/amazon-retail-arbitrage-business/

https://www.thebalancesmb.com/earn-usd18-to-usd25-an-hour-delivering-for-the-tech-giant-4174269

My other book on how to work from home:

**«Work from home: $10,000 per Month.
Proven Case Studies»:
https://www.amazon.com/dp/B07FQCF449**

**Did you like this book?
If you did, please give it a 5-star rating on
Amazon.**

Made in United States
Orlando, FL
27 May 2022

18256258R00017